Did you know that everyone has an aura, a field of energy surrounding them? The aura is a combination of our mind, body and spirit. When you look into a person's aura, your newfound knowledge can be used for healing, and for increased personal awareness. After reading *Aura: Understanding, Seeing and Healing*, you'll be able to see your own aura, and the aura of those around you.

Connie Islin has published many books on mysticism, healing, crystals and parapsychology. Her books about dream interpretation and numerology have become bestsellers, and have been translated into many languages. She lives in the U.S.A. and in Israel. She is a consultant and lecturer on mystical subjects and alternative medicine. This is her second book in English.

LITTLE **BIG** BOOK

of

Aura
Understanding, Seeing and Healing

by Connie Islin

Astrolog Publishing House

Astrolog Publishing House
P.O. Box 1123, Hod Hasharon 45111, Israel
Tel: 972-9-7412044
Fax: 972-9-7442714
E-Mail: info@astrolog.co.il
Astrolog Web Site: www.astrolog.co.il

ISBN 965-494-053-1

Published by Astrolog Publishing House 1998

Printed in Israel
10 9 8 7 6 5 4 3 2 1

History

An aura is the wreath of light surrounding an object that emits radiation. Testimonies to the existence of human auras and attempts to interpret them were already present in early writings: "...and surrounding his head was a crown of radiance... enveloping it unto two arms' lengths" (Book of Visions); "And when the priest neared his hand to the man, the radiant armor would be rent and the evil spirit would have a manner in which to go forth from him" (Sebilius).

The historical descriptions of human auras are almost identical to those of today. The difference between them lies in our ability to measure and quantify scientifically many phenomena which could not be explained in the past.

Today, scientists recognize the existence of electromagnetic and other types of radiation emitted by every body, whether living or "dead", and can indeed measure them precisely. Modern science allows us to calibrate the electromagnetic radiation that creates auras.

Radiation emitted by any body, be it animal, plant or mineral, may be measured. For example, the intensity of radiation emitted by a mineral tells us its age. Brain-waves, too, were a mystery impossible to quantify until the advent of modern science.

Today, there are visual aids that demonstrate how, by concentrating and using mental power, a person may change his brain-waves. In recent years, games have been developed which require the attachment of electrodes to the sides of player's head. As the player concentrates or relaxes, his changing brain-waves are monitored by the electrodes. On a screen in front of the player is a figure. If the player succeeds in directing his brain-waves appropriately - let us say, by freeing himelf from nervous tension and increasing his concentration - the figure will reach the target.

A significant breakthrough occurred a few decades ago as a result of the Kirlians' research, which for the first time enabled us both to photograph as well as actually view auras. All of a sudden, anyone could take a picture of his aura!

The Kirlians - a husband and wife team - worked in the former Soviet Union. In 1958,.

they discovered a method of photographing the aura, or the wreath of the aura, on the skin of the living body. The photograph is taken by means of high-voltage electricity, which imprints the picture on a metal sheet - *without the use of a camera lens!*

In the past, the existence of auras was subject to people's belief or skepticism, and only a few individuals could see them. Today, with the aid of Kirlian Photography or other means of measurement, anyone may see a map of his aura, or even of the colors in his aura.

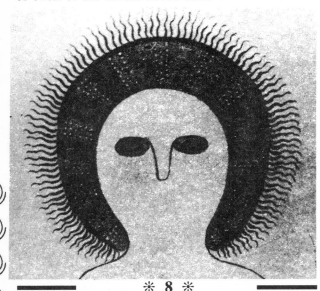

As opposed to other types of radiation, however, we do not know what human radiation or its source is, or how it can be influenced. We know how to affect it indirectly (for example, it is possible to "direct" it using breath control), but we do not yet have an unequivocal scientific explanation for its existence. Therefore, in order to examine it to the best of our ability, we have no choice but to gather snippets of available information and attempt to create a larger picture.

To this end, first and foremost, we must convince the reader that natural, everyday behavior testifies to the existence of auras and teaches us how to utilize them. If the reader is not a believer, we will try to "convert" him. And if he already is, we will enable him to reinforce his belief.

What is a "ray" or "radiation"?

Let us examine the ancient references to rays of light, as in "...Moses' face sent forth rays" (Exodus 34:35) or "And a brightness appeareth as the light; rays hath He at His side" (Habakkuk 3:4). Clearly, these citations refer to an inner light seen by others in the face of an individual.

There are many expressions describing

visible radiation emitted by the body. One may
speak of a woman who "radiates sexuality", about
someone who has erected an "invisible wall"
around him, or a person who spreads "blackness"
around him, etc. It is easy to mistake body
language for the aura surrounding someone.
When we talk about a person whose "face has
fallen", we are referring to his body language.
The confusion between the two might be due to
the fact that the aura and its dynamics constitute
an integral part of one's body language - a part
that cannot be seen, heard or smelled, but rather
felt through extrasensory perception.

A significant part of the aura's radiation
belongs to the individual's body language, but
not always. Occasionally, someone might appear
to be happy and light-hearted, though his aura
testifies to sadness and pain. Someone else might
present his body as a wall, rejecting any physical
contact, while his aura asks for intimacy and
warmth.

In Britain, tests were conducted on people
who could read auras, among them a few quite
famous readers. They were presented with about
20 people covered in identical white shrouds.
Auras are not influenced by identical clothing.

The readers were asked to identify the gender, age and skin color of the person in question. Out of 140 "readings" (the number of readers multiplied by the number of individuals), only seven answered all three questions correctly; 31 readings produced two out of three correct answers; and the rest were only random guesses. In other words, *body language has a significant influence.*

In this book we will try to ignore this factor, despite the fact that we are well aware of its importance.

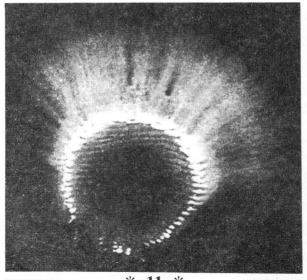

If we observe a group of people at a funeral, for example, the reader may identify the actual mourner by his aura: projected from the depths of his inner heart, mourning and sadness go beyond the conventionally acceptable body language of someone participating only superficially in the event.

From the point of view of human beings, auras have several characteristics. The radiation - the "beam" or "light" - is not identified as one of the five known senses. However, as with other human qualities, it is related to other aspects of the individual. Radiating sexual energy, for example, is expressed in the aura as well as in "inviting" body language, a gay and joyful voice and an attractive odor. Mourning radiates a "dark" aura, and is characterized by reserve and an inward withdrawal, a low, quiet voice, a strong body odor, etc. The aura is an integral part of the different body systems - all working together!

Each natural phenomenon has a goal or objective, general or specific. For example, the panda's curved claw is designed precisely in order to expose the bamboo bud that serves as his main source of food. If the claw is removed, the panda will starve!

The aura, too, possesses an objective and a

goal. Its spiritual objective is to preserve the spirit after the death of the body; its physical objective is to serve as a protective shield against cosmic radiation unknown to us. And perhaps the aura also serves as armor which encases the soul as it moves from one incarnation to another... or maybe it is a remnant of an unknown sixth sense?

If one believes in auras and recognizes their existence, it is much easier to study their shape, color, use and ways in which they might benefit us.

In order to examine the source of the aura and its meaning, we must elaborate on the subject.

First, let us make a random list of all we know about auras:

• People can indeed see auras. Period.

• Auras may be measured by means of certain instruments.

• Pictures of saints show auras surrounding their heads.

• The Bible is full of expressions testifying to the fact that the existence of auras or radiation was recognized in early times.

• Ancient drawings depict not only the aura, but its layers as well.

• The diminishing or absence of an aura attests to the end of the life cycle.

• Auras are an inherent part of health, which may be influenced by the diagnosis and treatment of auras.

• Auras change their colors, thickness and density throughout one's life.

• Anyone may see auras, especially people who are able to reach a highly concentrated awareness.

• It is possible to distinguish between the auras of a man, woman, child, animal or plant. In other words, different auras exist.

• Auras possess energy.

• When two auras make contact, they do not merge, though they may strengthen or weaken each other.

• Auras are not affected by other bodies.

• The individual is born with an aura, which crystallizes by the age of two. As time passes, it does change, but basically it remains identical to the birth aura.

Shapes of Auras

Descriptions of shapes of auras differ. At times, the differences between the various approaches and evidence are enormous. Sometimes, the descriptions are general; at others, they are as precise as a geographical diagram.

There are basic disagreements concerning the thickness of the aura on the surface of the human body. Some people describe the thickness as two to three centimeters (about an inch), while others claim that it is up to 30 centimeters (12 inches) thick. There are auras that are further away from the body; researchers define them as "spiritual auras" which are not visible, although they are known to exist.

Most approaches speak of auras close to the body, without an "insulating layer" of air between the body and the aura. A few place the aura at a distance of approximately three centimeters from the body.

Some people differentiate between the general body aura and the aura surrounding the head, or appearing above the crown in the shape of a ball. Some readers see the aura as a ball or egg-shaped object containing the human body, but most describe it as roughly outlining the contours of the body.

In some readings, the "center" of the aura, parallel to the upper chakras, is seen contained within the general framework of the aura surrounding the body.

An additional question addresses the structure of the aura: Is it composed of many layers, each with a different purpose, or is it a misty body surrounding the person?

The Aura Institute in the United States collected descriptions of over 7,000 auras examined by 80 readers. In addition, the Institute investigated about 130 auras using Kirlian photography and gathered approximately 30,000 descriptions from various drawings and writings.

The different approaches are well exemplified in the illustrations in this chapter. In addition, a basic diagram is included that may be used for mapping auras if you choose to try and see an aura on your own.

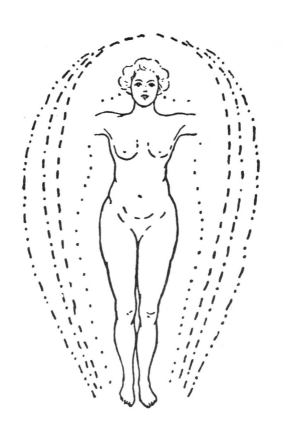

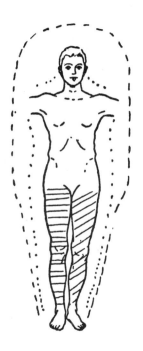

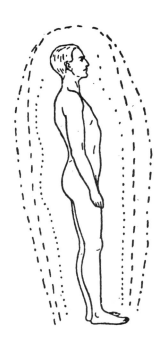

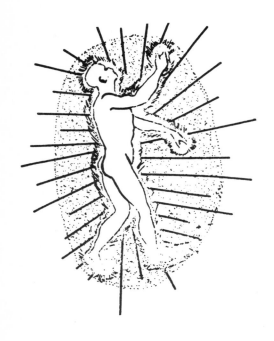

Try to sketch the outline of the aura you see in this diagram.

What are the characteristics of auras?

1. Their thickness reaches about 30 centimeters. Around the arms it is about 10 centimeters thick, while above the nape of the neck, for example, the aura may be as thick as 40 centimeters. The closer the aura is to the skin, the denser it is.

2. The aura does not disappear, nor can it be damaged. Even when we walk, our aura continues to exist under our feet, and when we wear a helmet, the aura remains above our head.

3. The aura assumes the shape of the particular body and it is therefore possible to distinguish the gender, weight and height of the individual.

4. The aura consists of many different colors blended together.

5. The aura is not uniform. There are sections that are misty, sections that are clearly layered, planes of color, etc.

6. Within the aura, there are empty, hole-like areas as well as concentrated rays forming a beam of light emitted by a specific part of the body. There are sphere-like aura masses within the web of the aura.

The main task of the reader of the aura is classifying the colors of the aura, distinguishing its shape and identifying holes and concentrations. This allows him to diagnose, monitor and treat human behavior.

7. A person's body and soul are reflected in the aura.

8. By working properly with the aura, one may repair it. This entails repairing the source of the damage.

9. The shape and colors of an aura may be photographed and sketched.

10. The aura we perceive reflects the body/spirit/soul. This is the aura we will discuss. (An additional aura, one we will not deal with, surrounds this aura. Known as the cosmic aura, it is connected solely to the astral body.)

Case Study

A British corporation owning a chain of supermarkets began to accumulate losses due to deficient management. Following attempts to remedy the situation by streamlining and reorganization, the management decided to send regional managers to an institute where auras were diagnosed.

The managers were unaware of the nature of the institute, which was further camouflaged by their participation in a management game. Two aura readers monitored the participants.

During the interactions between the managers, the readers discerned that the company's regional comptroller had an unusual aura. Above the nape of his neck and shoulders, his aura was full of brown spots, which did not disappear even during breaks in the game.

The aura indicated that the comptroller took the entire burden of responsibility upon himself, not trusting or cooperating with others. This created a great deal of tension between him and them, as this message was unconsciously transmitted to them. Because of his important position, the auras of the managers reflected acquiescence, submissiveness and reconciliation. In time, the auras of the other participants lost their red, orange and yellow colors - colors which characterize positive auras - and they became quiet, polite and listless.

There was a significant rise in the corporation's profits within as little as three months after the comptroller was fired.

Colors of Auras

In Japan, reading auras in situations that might appear foreign and strange to a Westerner is part of daily life.

For example, take the breeding of gamecocks for cockfighting - a very popular sport in Japan and the focus of a major gambling industry. The breeder sells the chicks to other breeders. Prior to the sale, aura readers ("those who see the inner spirit", in Japanese) examine the chicks. On each one they place a colored ribbon matching the color of its aura. The redder the aura, the stronger the fighting spirit and aggressiveness of the gamecock. The value of the gamecocks with the reddest ribbons is extremely high and may reach a few hundred dollars, while the value of those with pale red ribbons is merely a few dollars.

In Tokyo's fish market, as well, one might meet an aura reader drawing an aura for a few yen. These drawings are very popular, particularly among young couples who seek to find out about each other by means of the colors of their auras.

These are just two examples of the wondrous combination of the unfamiliar, unknown and mystical realms with everyday life in the Far East.

Remember that it is important that we understand what there is to see in an aura.

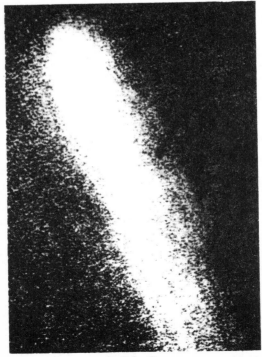

In principle, color is radiation, identical to the electromagnetic radiation of the aura, sound waves or other types of rays. When we see the colors of the aura, we are actually applying those colors to the qualities of the aura's radiation. The color reveals the texture and characteristics of the aura.

Although there is a full correlation between the aura's colors and its qualities, it is important to remember that the color serves as an intermediary, helping us to see the aura.

When discussing the colors of auras, we should note three important principles:

1. The environment influences the way the colors are perceived: if a blue object is placed on a yellow surface, the aura will appear green, but the green color is only as a result of distortion by the human eye!

In order to prevent such distortions, it is necessary to examine the aura against a neutral background. (Auras may also be seen in the dark, thereby completely neutralizing any distortion.)

2. Occasionally, a color-blind person may have to "correct" the color chart in order to interpret the colors of the aura correctly.

3. Hundreds of shades of colors (mostly greens, blues and reds) exist in auras. We will concentrate on the principal and most prominent basic colors.

The colors of the aura are not static; they change according to the state of the person at any given time.

Basic Colors of Auras

White Auras

In essence, white is life. A white aura exists in every living body. If we cut off a piece of a leaf and photograph it using Kirlian photography, we will see white around its cut edges, and white mixed with other colors around its other edges. A day later, the white color will disappear and mix with other colors, such as brown and gray, attesting to the fact that the imprint of life is fading.

A newborn baby has a pure white aura. During his life, the aura becomes filled with additional colors, but the white color is always present in the background or within the other colors.

In principle, a pure white aura signifies purity and health. A dull aura, or one that tends toward gray or brown, usually indicates health problems.

During times of transition in a person's life, such as birth or death, or in the case of a person with a highly developed ability for inner concentration, the aura may seem to shine with a sort of higher radiance (at birth), or to fade and disappear (at death).

It is quite easy to distinguish the white aura when the individual is naked and standing against a black background. However, it is very difficult to see it when the person is illuminated by a bright light or is wearing white garments and is standing against a colored background.

Black Auras

Black auras are in fact the lack of white ones. These auras, at times appearing as clumps of black areas on the outer surface of the body, indicate a serious disease or "dead" organ.

During times of transition of the white aura, the color black appears, but immediately disappears.

Usually, a black aura may only be seen on the naked body. Using Kirlian photography or other means of measurement, the black aura may be seen as dark brown.

Gray Auras

Gray auras are not a good sign. They signify danger and indicate that the white aura has been "injured".

Gray auras appear as a grid superimposed on other colors, weakening their positive qualities. The aura looks like gray smoke and it

is important to be able to identify it in order to purify it and improve the condition of the person. A headache, for example, is manifested in a gray aura surrounding the head. When the pain subsides, the gray aura disappears.

Gray auras are easily seen against a white background. Occasionally, they appear in the form of a spirit leaving the body via the different orifices - seven in the male body and eight in the female body.

Red Auras

Red auras come in many shades and are present in all living beings. In principle, the red aura indicates one's level of vitality. During certain periods, the red aura is more prominent (during pregnancy, battle or courtship, for example) and during others, it is pale and weak.

The red aura affects the circulatory and nervous systems.

The brighter the red color in the aura, the more energy and vitality the person enjoys. If the red is actually brownish-red or mixed with black spots, it indicates serious health disorders. A dirty, dark red aura signifies that the corresponding body part is malfunctioning or injured. Red combined with yellow, particularly

in the area of the loins, testifies to a "good soul".
Broken red areas indicate a weak nervous system.
Fiery red, especially around the eyes, mouth and
sexual organs (loins and breasts), signifies
arrogance and hypocrisy. Pink indicates a lack
of emotional maturity. It is difficult to find a
pure red aura, and therefore much skill is
required to assess the intensity and significance
of red auras.

Orange Auras

Some readers confuse reddish-yellow auras
with orange auras (the actual color of the fruit).
Orange is a positive color and indicates a
powerful aura, as well as a highly sexual one.

When the orange color is dark, muddy or
tending toward brown, it is a sign that the person
is not exploiting his talents. In addition, it
indicates health problems, particularly in parts of
the body concerned with liquids, such as the
kidneys and liver. In some instances, orange
auras appear as spots on another aura, especially
a green one. This indicates that the individual is
at odds with himself.

It is easy to examine orange auras when the
individual is naked, and they will almost always
appear in the area of the genitals and back. They

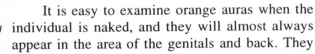

are also visible during sexual intercourse, but are not visible in bright sunlight.

Yellow Auras

Yellow auras are usually positive. They are commonly located in all body parts and present in all of us. When yellow auras appear around the head, they signify the spiritual halo with which religious teachers, spiritual people, saints and those with a very high level of self-awareness are endowed.

Pale yellow indicates a healthy spirit. If it is mixed with brown and appears "muddy", it suggests the existence of a spiritual defect in the person's soul. If the yellow aura is combined with a red one, it indicates difficulties in social adjustment, tension and nervousness. When a yellow aura appears together with a green one, it signifies medical problems related to the internal organs and glands. Two muddy yellow clouds above the individual's head are signs of a divided soul and split personality.

Yellow auras are mainly influenced by thought processes, and therefore the way to purify them is by making a spiritual effort to improve awareness.

Green Auras

Green auras are the most important for human beings with regard to health. "Holes" in the auras suggest possible health problems. They serve as a protective armor surrounding the body, and if they are breached, they allow the enemy to thrust his sword directly into living flesh!

If a green aura appears in combination with pale yellow, each layer separate but overlapping, it indicates the highest level of spiritual illumination. (However, when the yellow aura is stuck to the green, it weakens the green one.)

A bluish-green aura signifies that the person is trying to exert a positive influence on society. If the aura tends toward green-blue, it indicates that he is very trustworthy. A green aura tending toward yellow warns that the person is hypo-critical.

It is quite easy to influence a green aura by means of external treatment.

Blue Auras

The blue aura is the spiritual aura. It does not appear as armor, but as blue smoke. It is indicative of the power of spirit and soul.

Blue auras are not continuous. We see signs

of them around the mouth, loins, stomach and nape of the neck. They are difficult to discern, and, at times, mistakenly identified, especially against a dark background.

Purple Auras (Indigo)

Purple auras usually indicate the dedication of the body to the needs of the soul - as in the case of deeply religious persons or those devoted to some sort of ideology. If the purple aura tends toward red or pink, it is an indication of hypersensitivity. When it tends toward shining blue, it means that the person has problems with the heart and digestive system. A purple aura usually resembles a heavy overcoat thrown over the shoulders.

Brown Auras

Brown auras usually appear in the form of stains in other auras. A brown aura always indicates damage to other auras and warns of disease, a bad heart, etc. When a person is completely surrounded by a brown aura, it is a sign that his heart is congenitally weak or that he is about to die. Treatment to remove a brown aura must be carried out by an experienced reader.

How do we see an aura?

With great difficulty!

In order to be able to see an aura, a lot of practice coupled with natural talent is required. It is estimated that about one third of all people see auras following limited training, another third see auras after extensive training, and the final third are unable to see them.

There are two requirements for being able to see auras: inner centering and external vision.

The term "inner centering" refers to the mental state of the observer. First and foremost, he must be convinced that he is able to see auras. Second, he must be relaxed, but not too relaxed! Finally, he must use his external sense of sight. The eyes are the tools used for seeing auras.

This is not the place to teach centering and relaxation techniques. If a person is interested in seeing and understanding auras, he must prepare himself on his own.

However, we will elaborate upon how to practice developing vision which is capable of seeing auras.

In order to see the colors of the aura, we must first "dress" the mysterious aura in something familiar to the human eye. The question remains: Can the eye voluntarily imagine a color?

Take a moment to remember the days when we had black and white TV sets at home. During breaks between broadcasts, the test pattern - a circle with the names of the different stations - would appear. If you looked at the black and white circle for a while, you would begin to see flickering colors - waves created by the eye. If you were able to see colors on a black and white screen, you will be able to see auras.

We will now present a tool that will enable you to practice on your own. Please follow the instructions exactly.

On the following page is a black and white "optical" drawing with a row of numbers at the bottom. Place the page on a white wall and stand exactly three meters (about three yards) from the wall. Try to identify the numbers while keeping both eyes open. If you succeed, photocopy the drawing (1:1) and use it for the exercise.

If you cannot identify the numbers, move closer to the wall until you can. Now measure your distance from the wall. The difference between three meters and the place where you are standing is the proportion according to which you must enlarge the drawing when photo-copying.

385023

For example: Let us say that you succeeded in seeing the numbers from a distance of two meters. The proportion that must be taken into account is 3:2. In other words, you must enlarge the drawing by photocopying it at 150% of its size.

Some people may need to distance themselves more than three meters from the wall in order to see the numbers. In this case, move backwards, but do not enlarge the drawing. Photocopy it at 1:1.

It is important that the wall be completely white and stretch a meter and a half to each side of the drawing (without pictures or furniture). In addition, it is crucial that the floor be of neutral colors and not have colored tiles or carpets.

Next, concentrate on the center of the drawing while in a state of relaxation. Make sure you are breathing rhythmically. Do not, under any circumstances, hold your breath. Keep looking for about 90 seconds, not more. If you see colors flickering within a short period of time, you will be able to see auras! If you do not see them, repeat the exercise after a *three-hour break!*

Even if you have seen flickering colors, repeat the exercise once a day in order to maintain the ability you have developed to see auras.

The second exercise requires five identical sealed black boxes or five identical black envelopes. Next, find five objects, four of one color and the fifth of a different color. It is best to combine red and green objects, as they are easiest to see.

It is important to note that a warm body emits auras better than a cold one. Therefore, it is advisable to choose objects that are "alive", such as flower, leaves or vegetables.

Remember that you want to see an aura, and the color of the aura is not necessarily the color of the object. However, in the case of inanimate objects, there is a 70-80% correlation between their visible color and the color of their aura; when dealing with plants, the correlation reaches 70%.

Let us assume that we have chosen four ripe cherry tomatoes (small ones) and one olive. Now, ask someone to put one of the five objects in each box without your knowledge. Your task is to "see" the colors of the auras, which in this instance will radiate out of the black boxes.

Random guessing will allow you to identify where the olive is one out of five times (20% of the time). Using your inner, hidden vision, you may increase this rate to 30%. We claim that by means of seeing auras, you will be able to identify the olive with certainty.

After preparing the experiment, center yourself and enter into a relaxed state, trying to see the color emitted from the box before your very eyes! It is difficult. Concentrate on one color - let us say green. If you do not see green, do not guess! Try again.

Following a short trial period, you will be able to find (without guessing) where the olive is three out of five times. That's a lot! As time goes by, you will discover that as you move the boxes further away from one another, your ability will improve, even reaching absolute knowledge!

Having completed this exercise, we will now move on to seeing human auras.

How do we ascertain who is an "aura reader" and who is a charlatan?

Some "aura readers" describe colored wings growing out of the back or horns above the head, after a brief glance at the client. Such a detailed aura reading is very rare. Usually, those who see auras only see sparks or clouds of color, and not defined outlines and shapes.

You may test if the reader can actually see your aura or if he is a fraud. Seeing auras involves seeing color emitted by a living body, in other words, warmer than 10°C. When you wear a garment or place a piece of paper in your pocket, it warms up, and from the point of view of the aura, is a living object, i.e., it emits color. Therefore, try asking the reader what the color of your underwear or the card in your pocket is, etc.

Can you see auras?

To begin with, attempt to see your own aura. The hands and feet are aura-rich organs - meaning that aura "pours" out of them in large masses. The only organs that possess a larger concentration of aura relative to area are the genitals.

Spread your hands out in front of you against a white or black background. Now concentrate your vision on the back of your open hand. After some effort, you will be able to identify sparks of color, particularly between the fingers. This, indeed, is your aura!

You may try a similar exercise with another person who is comfortable with you in the nude. Ask him to lie naked on a white sheet. Your eyes should be at the level of his feet when you are a short distance from the bed. Try to see the entire length of the body. After a while, you will begin to see different colors that look as if they are rising from his body like hot steam.

The Aura and Healing

What is healing?
Healing refers to cure.

The aura is an integral part of healing, and healing is an integral part of the aura.

Just as a light bulb is meaningless without electricity, so healing is meaningless without the aura!

The aura is made up of electromagnetic fields. Each of these fields contains two forces or layers - the electric force and the magnetic force. Both are activated by contact between particles and each has the ability to create an electromagnetic field.

In the case of the human body, complex biochemical activity takes place throughout one's entire lifespan. The electric currents are transmitted from cell to cell, connecting one cell to the other. Through their movement they create electromagnetic fields.

Electric and magnetic movements may be seen when brain-waves are recorded, for example.

Our entire nervous system operates by means of electronic signals. Furthermore, we know that a human heart may be repeatedly reactivated with electric shocks. Pacemakers send continuous electronic signals to the heart, etc.

Each living being, mineral or plant possesses an electromagnetic field. Each object has a different quality of particle activity, ranging from zero to vital, lively activity.

The aim of healing is to bring the living body - in this case, the human body - to the optimal level of particle activity, producing the optimal electromagnetic field.

The sheath of the aura, or the enveloping electromagnetic field, matches the shape of the body. Nevertheless, electromagnetic fields exist independently! This fact is highly significant. In the past, however, it was contested. Some claimed that the aura overlapped the human body, meaning that if, for example, someone's leg was amputated, the aura would display the contours of the amputated leg, similar to a shadow. Others believed that the aura depicted the individual's *nature* and would always reflect both whole legs - according to the way it should be.

Two proofs support the second opinion:

The first is phantom pain, which occurs when people have had a limb amputated; it seems as if the limb still hurts, even after the amputation. This pain proves that something exists in place of the severed limb.

The second proof came to light following an experiment conducted by the Kirlians, in which they photographed a damaged leaf against a metal plate. In the photograph, the aura of the damaged leaf was whole! In the damaged area was a white, misty aura, different from the rest of the aura. In subsequent experiments conducted on leaves or animals with severed limbs, the missing areas always appear complete with a white aura.

We conclude that *the aura reflects the complete person, not only the body, spirit or soul that are affected by the electromagnetic field. It does not matter what happens to the individual... his aura will reflect his true nature!*

Auras may be *seen* if one develops the ability to read auras, in other words, to see electromagnetic waves and fields; they may be *photographed* using Kirlian photography, and they may be *felt* with the hand, which is able to sense the tingling of the electromagnetic field.

Nowadays, electromagnetic fields are measured in the atmosphere and in space, though many phenomena associated with them, such as the *aurora borealis*, were known in the past.

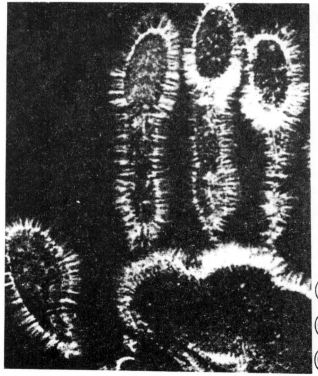

It is probable that in the not-so-distant future, it will be possible to measure auras with the same tools used today to examine brain-waves or to perform ultrasound examinations.

How are auras connected with healing?

Remember that auras plainly reflect *a person's true state* - his physical, mental and spiritual health! Through the use of auras, we will be able to diagnose which of the above require healing.

Generally speaking, a strong, thick, shining aura always indicates a healthier person than a weak, thin, dull one does.

It is important to note that the aura is constantly changing according to both internal and external influences.

This endless process of alteration is liable to create not only changes in the strength and thickness of the aura, but actual tears or holes. The human aura will then attempt to close these holes, in the same manner that a wound congeals.

Each body has an aura of a different thickness, determined by its intensity. The earth's aura is about 50,000 miles thick. The aura of an average person extends some dozens of centimeters away from the skin. The aura of a leaf is about half a centimeter away from the leaf.

In any case, *a body's aura extends to where the electromagnetic aura of the environment balances the aura of the body.*

As the type of radiation under discussion is electromagnetic by nature, the most efficient way to receive these waves is via satellite dish. Therefore, it is clear why, during healing, it is specifically the hand that serves as the medium for receiving and sending energy involving electromagnetic waves. The shape of the hand, slightly concave, greatly resembles the shape of the satellite dish used to receive energy waves.

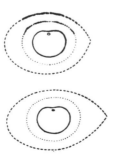

Cross-sections of various auras

Locating Auras

Each person exists within an egg-shaped aura which surrounds him. The electromagnetic aura occupies two-thirds of the volume and the person himself, another third - the same proportion as that of water and solid materials in the human body.

As mentioned above, this aura is influenced by internal and external factors, for better or for worse. Natural cure, or healing, is the way to influence the aura externally.

In order to locate the electromagnetic aura of another person, the healer must prepare his equipment, in other words, his two hands. His hands must be clean and the blood must be allowed to flow to them, thus clearing energy blockages and stoppages. This is done by alternately clenching fists and opening and stretching the hands. Following this step, the hands are rubbed together and the fingers are firmly massaged by the thumbs. When the palms are hot, they are ready to give a treatment. Now the hands are shaken (as if shaking off water).

In order to examine a person's energy field, he must be seated on a chair with a straight back, his heels below his coccyx and his knees apart.

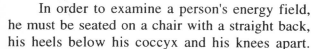

His hands must be placed on his thighs. The healer stands two steps away from the seated person. Remember: During the treatment, contact is established between the healer's aura and the patient's aura, as each person's aura extends to a radius of about one foot. However, this contact is not felt. Only when the healer directly touches the sheath of the patient's aura with his palms will he sense the first reaction.

Touching the aura transmits two sensations to the experienced healer: One is the feeling of intermittent, tingling heat-waves, and the other is the sense of touching something soft that recedes when touched with the hand. When the healer feels these sensations, he must move his hands to the left and right, as if mapping the sheath of radiation. He must constantly observe the seated person, as he too reacts when his aura is touched, for example, by blinking or by wincing involuntarily.

What, in fact, is healing?

Occasionally, a person's aura is damaged and dirtied. Stains may appear, as well as disruptions or stoppages in the electromagnetic flow. When the healer passes his hand over the damaged or dirty area, it cleanses the area and renews the flow of good energy.

The first step in healing is, then, an external cleansing of the aura. This cleansing also serves as a preventive treatment. If the aura is cleansed on a regular basis, it will not accumulate amounts of dirt that result in disease.

The sheath of the aura is indeed located about a foot from the body. However, the most effective treatment occurs when the aura is compressed, pressing as close to the body as possible, and massaged while touching the skin. When the treatment is completed, the aura expands - stronger and more intact - to its full dimensions.

Breathing the aura

Exhaling, inhaling and charging auras

Auras are influenced by other intervening auras. In other words, if we describe the aura in simple terms, it is like a cloud or mass of vapor. As such, it is affected by energy flows with similar characteristics. Therefore, if we blow on the aura, or pass a hand over it (taking into consideration the fact that surrounding the hand is a strong concentration of aura), it will change its form, and whirlpools and flows of aura will form at the point where the auras make contact. If, for example, we pass a completely different type of material through it, say a needle, the needle will pass through the aura as if it did not exist.

It is important to understand that the study of the aura surrounding the human being is similar to the study of airflow, which exists, for example, around an airplane at take-off. In both cases, with the use of simple tools, the different flows may be observed.

Aura readers are aware of the fact that a

strong and energetic concentration of aura is found around the mouth, one that is in constant motion. The mouth is the meeting place between the inner aura and the outer aura. It actually constitutes the gateway through which the aura leaves and enters the body easily. That is, the mouth is the main transmitter of aura into and out of the body. During times of pressure or effort (such as running), we utilize our full *oral* respiratory ability and hence provide "first aid" to the aura mass.

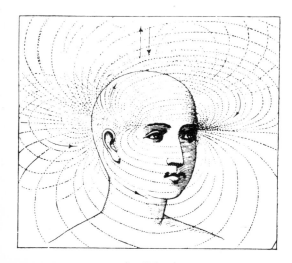

Regular inhalation and exhalation creates a constantly-moving whirlpool of aura surrounding the mouth. This whirlpool is easily moved or directed elsewhere by exhaling, when one desires to direct it outwards, far from the mouth; or alternatively, by inhaling, when one wants to draw energy into the body. In other words, if we seek to activate the aura in a focused and immediate manner, we have only to direct the respiratory whirlpool of the aura to the desired place and move it by using the flow of the aura, which is part of the process of inhaling and exhaling.

If we wish to push a car, we have to expend a greater amount of energy for the first push than for the second or third. It is the same with the aura. It is easier to move an aura in motion than to move an aura that is "frozen" or static.

Practitioners who engage in an optimal form of yoga, letting their body sink into a deep, death-like sleep that brings biological processes to a standstill, display an aura resembling an unmoving metallic surface. However, the aura at the mouth continues to move, albeit slowly.

If we observe the behavior of people who have been injured or wounded, we will notice that many tend to blow on the wound. Children ask their mothers to kiss the place that hurts. Although these actions are intuitive, they make sense. Unwittingly, we heal the blow or the wound by mending the sheath of the aura. We offer first aid using the whirlpool of the aura and directing it to the injured spot.

A common brand of treatment or cure utilizing the aura is a process in which the healer blows on the patient's body and on the injured organ (usually by blowing on the appropriate chakra).

Exhaling the aura can serve as "first aid" for an aura in need of repair. In order to apply this technique, one must focus one's mind, enter into a state of relaxation (if one is not in a relaxed state of consciousness, it is impossible to work with the aura, or even see it) and gently exhale a flow of aura on to the damaged area of the aura requiring treatment.

With the help of this exhalation, energy is directed to the damaged area and absorbed by the aura, which is consequently repaired.

Occasionally, exhaling the aura is done unconsciously. Take, for example, basketball, tennis or football players who constantly use their hands during a game. We often see them

exhaling briefly on their fingers! They unconsciously take advantage of their aura, strength-
ening it in order to improve their performance.
Similarly, we frequently see soccer players
shaking their feet in order to remove a "bad" or
tired aura from their bodies.

In order to exhale the aura, the individual
must be familiar with his breathing. Correct
breathing brings a flow of air into the body,
charges it with the inner aura, and sends it back -
now charged with his aura - to the energy
whirlpool. If the breathing is not correct, the
breath will not be charged, and it will therefore
not be possible to exhale the aura or reap its
benefits.

Inhaling the aura is directed at the person
himself. Any person who wants to mend his aura
from within, thoroughly and rapidly, must learn
this type of breathing. In principle, inhaling the
aura draws the aura's energy whirlpool, located
near the mouth, into the body.

First, it must be noted that correct breathing
is the basis for inhaling the aura. Only after we
are aware of the proper breathing technique will
we be able to perform correct and effective
inhalation of the aura. We must draw the energy

whirlpool into the body in one continuous breath, taking a large amount of air into the lungs. The mind and the inner eye must be focused on a large ball of aura energy, moving in front of the mouth with every inhalation and exhalation. Even if you do not see it with your eyes, *see it in your mind!*

Now, exhale slowly and inhale deeply through the mouth. The ball of aura energy enters the body with the inhalation. Next, hold the breath and absorb the aura into the body. Feel the energy it contains. Slowly exhale the air once again together with the aura that was retained inside.

The ball of aura energy will return to its position in the sheath of the aura in front of the mouth, but will now have a different color, less energy, and will occasionally be smaller.

Repeat this exercise six to eight times, not more. It may be performed while standing or sitting, but never while lying down! (Exhaling the aura may be done in any position.) Following this process, a mild feeling of dizziness might be experienced. It is therefore desirable to practice in a place where there is no danger of falling.

Charging the Aura

The preliminary process of charging an aura is of the utmost significance. In fact, *inhaling the aura without charging the energy ball beforehand with the appropriate type or color of aura is not effective.*

In order to mend the inner aura, the energy ball must be charged with a color appropriate to restoring inner auras, and only then inhaled. If the individual is depressed, for example, the energy ball will contain shades of dark brown. If this type of energy ball is inhaled, not only will it not be beneficial, but it might even be harmful.

How can the ball of aura energy be charged with an appropriate color?

First, the aura must be examined with the eyes or the inner eye. In view of the fact that such an examination concerns the person himself, it is reasonable to assume that he knows the color of his aura and that it will be easy for him to identify which color is presently missing. (If he cannot perform the identification alone, he should seek assistance from someone who sees auras or from a healer.)

After having identified the missing color, the person in question must use his powers of imagination. Let us assume that he needs the color green in order to mend the inner aura - a process that immediately affects the outer aura. He must first focus his mind and imagine a green aura. He may, for example, imagine himself in a green forest. Next, he must reduce the image to the color green alone and concentrate on the color itself. In so doing, he should imagine the color within a large green ball, decreasing in size until it becomes a small green ball suspended right in front of his eyes. Using his imagination again, he must bring the green ball to the ball of aura energy in front of his mouth. The energy ball will now change as if by magic. The whirlpool will be different.

Now, the person should inhale the *restored* ball of aura energy and *draw from it the missing color*. Charging an aura will undeniably improve the benefits in inhaling it.

The aura and the tombs of the Pharaohs

There are several aura stories in which the elements of luck or surprise play a crucial role...

In a well-known museum in London, there are dozens of mummies - the preserved bodies of the Egyptian Pharaohs - taken from the tombs of the Pharaohs. In order to preserve the mummies for a long time in the optimal way, it is important that the site of the exhibits be carefully chosen. Temperature, humidity, radiation and air quality, as well as other conditions, must be monitored daily. Visits by the public, room temperature, etc., are regulated according to the results.

During the process of measuring energy in a hall containing three mummies, three concentrations of energy were discovered, using a technique similar to Kirlian photography. Upon examination, it was thought that the spotlights illuminating the mummies constituted the source of the energy concentrations. Later, the exhibition was changed and the mummies were moved into a corner of the room. Surprisingly, the energy concentrations moved to the corner as well! However, the spotlights remained in their original position...

Out of curiosity, a researcher by the name of Alvin Props decided to check this strange aberration. He used the same technique to photograph the 14 mummies in the museum, as well as 40 additional objects, some of them organic, from the same historical period, which he used as a control group. He determined that the energy concentration surrounding the mummies was much more intense (up to 80 times stronger) than that surrounding the other objects. We know that a living body possesses energy, or an aura, which subsides after death. However, the mummies displayed a concentration of energy or aura beyond any margin of error!

Props pursued his research and photographed eight additional mummies in England, the United States and other countries. He also photographed 16 non-Egyptian mummies from China, Peru and Italy.

The results were conclusive. The auras of the Egyptian mummies were stronger and different from the other mummies. The latter had auras similar to the "regular" aura as seen in the photographs of the 40 control objects.

Is it possible that the mysterious, lengthy, and expensive Egyptian mummification process was aimed at preserving the life force after death?

Props also discovered that the aura of the Egyptian mummies was shaped like a baby's body in the fetal position, that is, on its side with its feet curled to its stomach, the hands protecting the chest.

The strange thing is that the shape of the aura described above reflects the burial customs of the Canaanites, while the Egyptians tended to bury their dead lying flat on their backs!

Is there a reason for this?

Later in his study, following concerted efforts, Props succeeded in obtaining permission to expose three mummies. He unraveled their wrappings and cleaned the limbs. Next, he photographed them with Kirlian and energetic photography techniques - a kind of photograph that reveals the aura.

The results of the two techniques matched almost completely. To his surprise, the contours of the familiar and regular aura of the human body had assumed the shape of a fetus. Most astonishing was the fact that the lines of the "new" aura were perfect, hermetically sealed, as if preserving the energy or aura of the mummified body!

The ancient Egyptians believed in the resurrection of the dead, as well as in the idea that the spirit which left the body at death hovered above the remains of the physical body; it was that spirit which would return to the body at the time of resurrection. If a body was kept under "appropriate" conditions, in other words, in a coffin or tomb, the spirit would return to it rapidly. If the spirit wandered and the corpse was not preserved properly, there was a risk that the spirit would not return to the body.

Is the fact that the aura arranged itself in a position ideal for preserving the life force, proof that the ancient Egyptians indeed succeeded in their endeavor? Is a mummified body more alive than another corpse?

Alvin Props' conclusion was: Yes!

The study of auras and color therapy

In certain cultures, including Western culture, there is a complete dichotomy between conventional medicine and alternative medicine, which is closer to mysticism. And then there are cultures, such as that of China, where the two branches of medicine are close to each other. Usually there are interactions between the two fields, with one indeed influencing the other.

One of the areas in which there is a strong and surprising relationship between the two is color. Since the time when the Kirlians succeeded in photographing auras clearly, science has developed enormously, and today there are scanners and imaging devices which are able to identify the aura or electromagnetic energy of each and every cell. The most developed field connecting mysticism and science today is that of color therapy.

In addition, medical science has verified that there is a definite connection between mental disturbances and physical problems.

It is well known that color exerts a strong spiritual influence on human beings, their feelings, moods, etc. And so, if we influence the mind by changing colors, will the body be affected as well? It turns out that the answer is positive and easily proved.

For example, it is well known that the color red inspires love. The aura becomes red and subsequently physical traits change as well. There is a change in blood pressure and pulse rate, the cheeks become flushed, etc.

Bright yellow causes the aura to turn yellow and there is strong pressure on the bladder.

Dark purple or blue affects the color of the aura, causing the blood flow to slow down; occasionally there is pressure on the temples.

The healer, in his attempt to influence the aura, operates in three stages:

First, he concentrates on the patient and reads the vibrations (and colors) of his aura.

Second, within his body, he creates a wave of concentrated colored energy suited to the patient's aura but originating in the healer's.

Third, he influences the patient's aura, and in this way repairs the aura, spirit and physical body of the patient.

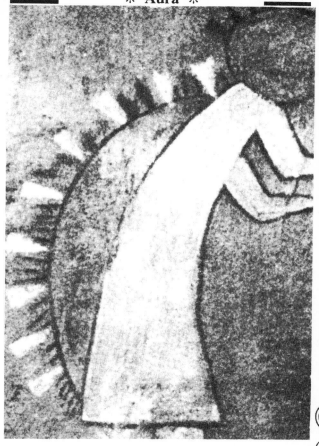

Waves of aura leaving the body.

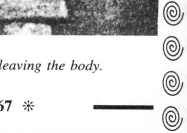

It is important to understand that this is not a "material" process, but rather a mental and spiritual one. *There is no use of light or color mediating between the healer and the person being treated.*

The beginning of the 20th century marked the advent of the interaction between mysticism and science. According to researchers, a "magnetic atmosphere" influenced by thought, including thoughts of color, surrounds human beings and the living body.

Researchers such as White, Kilner and Bagnall and others laid the foundations for the study of auras, color and their medicinal use decades before physicians and scientists proved these same assumptions scientifically!

Following the discovery of aura photography, researchers performed other experiments using colored plates in place of metal plates, and succeeded in obtaining colored auras. The Kirlians discovered that in each part of the skin or body, a different color dominates the aura. This color can never be exactly duplicated, even if two photographs are taken one after the other. According to them, we can assume that mental influence of any kind changes the color of the aura during the period between photographs.

They believed that this is a huge field for medical research and the diagnosis of diseases.

Today, with the aid of instruments that scan the waves and electromagnetic energy of the body, it is possible to identify the aura, layer by layer, without the use of optical lenses. By means of aura photographs of the body, any aura reader or healer can be asked to diagnose a person's state of health and recommend appropriate treatment.

In recent years, two new areas of knowledge have developed, influencing human awareness and creating a growing interest in auras. The first is meditation or relaxation in all its forms, as relaxation helps us to see auras.

A person seeking to improve his physical and mental health with the help of meditation, in fact applies spiritual power to the body. Success is seen in the changes in the shape and color of the aura.

The second area is the growing use of hallucinogenic drugs, medicines and plants, which occasionally help the user to see auras. Hallucinogens can induce the sighting of auras, as well as cause sharp and extreme changes in the user's aura. They mostly work to increase people's awareness of the presence of human auras. Utilizing mental powers to influence auras is one of the ways to give up using hallucinogenic drugs.